LEGENDS OF

NEW ORLEANS

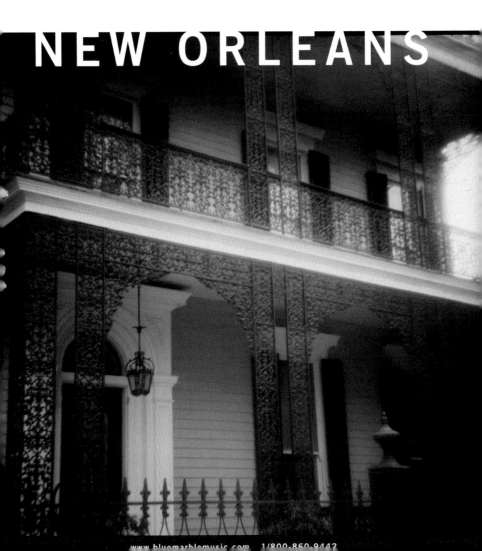

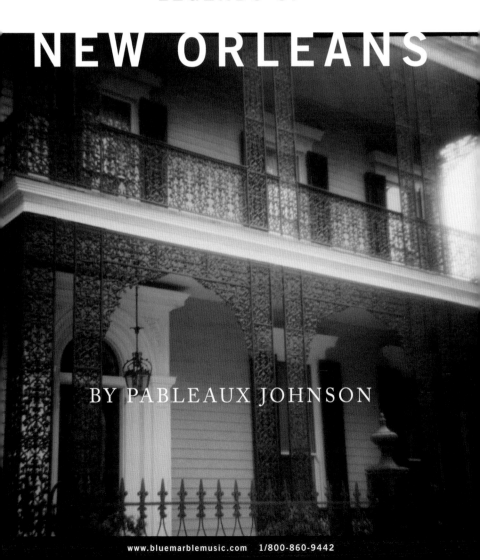

LEGENDS OF
NEW ORLEANS

BY PABLEAUX JOHNSON

www.bluemarblemusic.com   1/800-860-9442

WHERE WE ARE HEADED

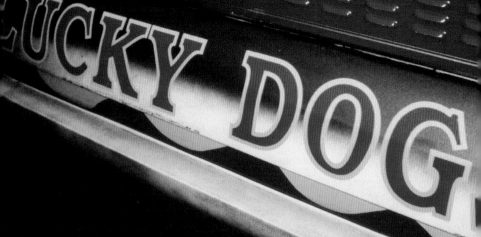

REG. HOT DOG: 3.25
a meat hot dog w/chili, mustard.

1/4 lb. SMOKED SAUSAGE: 4.25
Chili, mustard, onions.

CREOLE SAUSAGE: 4.25
Chili, mustard, onions.

SOFT DRINKS:
20 ounce bottle   2.00
                    Tax Included

LUCKY DOG

Before you get too far in collecting Blue Marble's music and guidebooks, I should confess something right from the start. I've always felt more comfortable in legendary dive joints than trendy hot spots. The contented, unhurried confidence of the people that run these places and the stories gathered over long-running histories ease my bones when I'm in their space.

So the music and guidebooks in our *Great Destinations Series* will focus on established, legendary 'institutions' that drench you in the richness of these great cultures of the world.

May the music you hear and the discoveries you make in New Orleans enrich your life. That is our goal at Blue Marble.

Steve Stone

Founder
Blue Marble

P.S. Even the purest intentions of cultural enlightenment can suffer a breakdown on Bourbon Street. If this happens to you, embrace the lost plot, yell "Hey weenie man!" and belly up to a loaded Lucky Dog – taking comfort that Jimmy Buffett probably sucked down hundreds of them during his early days soaking up New Orleans' music in the French Quarter.

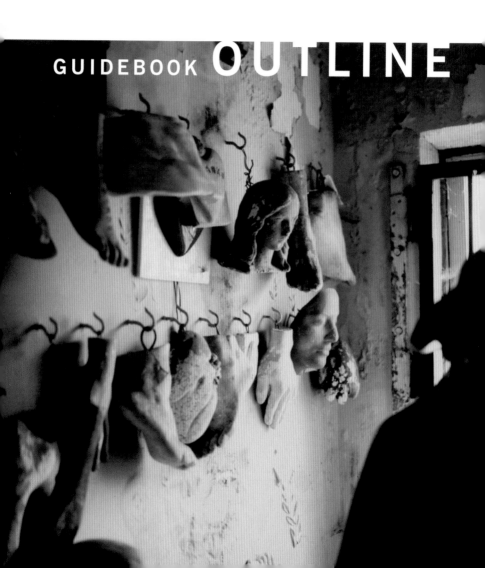

GUIDEBOOK OUTLINE

LEGENDS OF NEW ORLEANS

section		page
1	Getting Your Bearings	1
	The History	3
	European Influences	4
	African Influences	6
	The Neighborhoods	9
2	Music Legends	22
3	Food & Drink	36
4	The Classics	46
	Hotels	47
	Bars and Music Venues	49
5	Festival Schedule	50
6	Additional Resources	52
7	Credits	54

GETTING YOUR BEARINGS

Funky, exotic and just a little bit mysterious, New Orleans proudly wears the crown of "the least American of American cities." Enthusiastic tourists flock to the city every year for its infamous and decadent Mardi Gras and for the revelry in the well-known French Quarter.

More experienced visitors to New Orleans usually arrive seeking a different experience – one that reaches deeper into the culture of the fascinating metropolis. Looking past the Quarter, these visitors search out the city's sweet secret spots and dive head first into New Orleans' vibrant neighborhood cultures.

Legends of New Orleans has been designed for this type of visit. So for those seeking a New Orleans beyond Bourbon Street, the best place to begin is with a little history and a tour of the city's neighborhoods.

THE HISTORY

Ever since the French explorer De La Salle claimed the Mississippi River in 1682, European colonial powers clamored to dominate trade on the New World's inland waterways. Rivers from Kentucky to the promising Far West flowed into the mighty Mississippi, and Europeans fought to control the strategically critical 'end of the line'.

New Orleans came to life in the early 1700's as the Mississippi's largest downstream trading center and a major oceangoing port. Throughout nearly 300-years of intervening history, far-reaching cultures from around the world have mixed on the docks and in the city's streets, creating a uniquely vibrant urban culture that simply could not have developed anywhere else in the world.

EUROPEAN INFLUENCES

THE FRENCH

The French founded New Orleans in 1718 and in doing so, set a cultural tone that still survives in modern times. The original French Quarter (also called the Vieux Carré) was the city's first settlement and the center of French colonial culture in the years that followed. With powerful initial ties to their continental motherland, the French settlers and their descendents (known over time as **French Creoles**) adapted much of their Catholic home culture to the New World environment.

THE SPANISH

Though the city fell under Spanish control from 1762 to 1800, their colonial administrators never achieved real dominance over the entrenched French Creole communities. During their relatively short term of power, the Spanish oversaw the rebuilding of the city after two devastating fires ripped through the Quarter in 1788 and 1794. Much of the architectural brickwork in the Vieux Carré largely reflects a Spanish attempt to minimize fire hazard.

THE ACADIANS

Refugees from the French Canadian maritime province of Acadie, now Nova Scotia, were lured during the early years of Spanish rule with promises of land grants in the bayou country outside New Orleans. Expelled from Acadie by the British – the Acadians looked promising to the Catholic Spaniards, who valued the refugees for frontier experience and religious compatibility. The Acadians eventually built their own communities in the rural wetlands and coastal plains west of the city. Over time, this group became better known as the **Cajuns**, an American corruption of the term "Acadians."

THE AMERICANS

After a brief three-year return to French control starting in 1800, then-emperor Napoleon ceded control of New Orleans and its huge watershed to the Americans in 1803. Nine years later, the territory of Louisiana achieved statehood and New Orleans fell under American control.

THE GERMANS, IRISH AND ITALIANS

During the nineteenth century, a flood of European immigrants arrived and helped build the city's port and intricate levee system. Early German settlers populated the nearby Cote des Allemands, or German Coast. Irish immigrants fled their homeland and became an important force in New Orleans' working class, and Italians from Sicily arrived to establish their own strong neighborhood communities.

AFRICAN INFLUENCES

SLAVERY

Prior to the Civil War, New Orleans' commercial links to the upriver planta-
tions made it an active center for the American slave trade. Africans captured
from their continent's western coast were shipped to New Orleans via
Caribbean ports, where they were sold into slave labor.

The severe hardships and restrictions of slavery silenced much of the
Africans' culture in the new world. One great exception to this rule was the
Code Noir. In the early days of French rule, a colonial Code Noir (Black
Code) prohibited Sunday labor and allowed the slaves to play drums in a
prescribed section of New Orleans called Congo Square (modern-day Louis
Armstrong Park). The goal of the Code Noir was to push slaves toward
Catholicism, but in doing so, the code promoted cultural and linguistic conti-
nuity among the slaves and provided fertile ground for complex rhythms of
later New Orleans music.

CREOLES

The common French practice of split households and "slave mistresses" resulted in the development of thriving mixed-race communities who called themselves, confusingly enough, **Creoles**. Elaborate social rules and strata governed the lives of French-speaking Creoles, including a lineage system based on measuring a person's "African blood."

CARIBBEAN

A successful revolt of Haiti's African slaves in the late 1790s brought an influx of freed slaves to New Orleans, where they lived as gens des coleur libres (free people of color). Some of these freed immigrants traveled to rural Louisiana and created yet another branch on the Creole tree – **the South Louisiana Creoles**. This term generally describes outlying French-speaking black communities in Cajun country. Their traditional music was the basis of modern zydeco.

THE NEIGHBORHOODS

Getting your physical bearings in New Orleans isn't easy, especially given an often-confusing layout of the city's streets. New Orleans' byzantine urban plan hugs the broad curve of the river – making traditional compass directions nearly useless when giving directions. When locals describe a location, they're likely to replace "North, South, East and West" with "towards the lake, to the river, downtown and uptown."

Although New Orleans was born in the French Quarter, the magic of the modern-day city often lies in the neighborhoods beyond the well-defined Vieux Carré. If you want to stay ahead of Quarter-bound tourist throngs, the first (and best) step is to learn a bit about the other neighborhoods. Because, any local will tell you, it is in these less-touristy areas that you'll find New Orleans' hidden gems and hangouts.

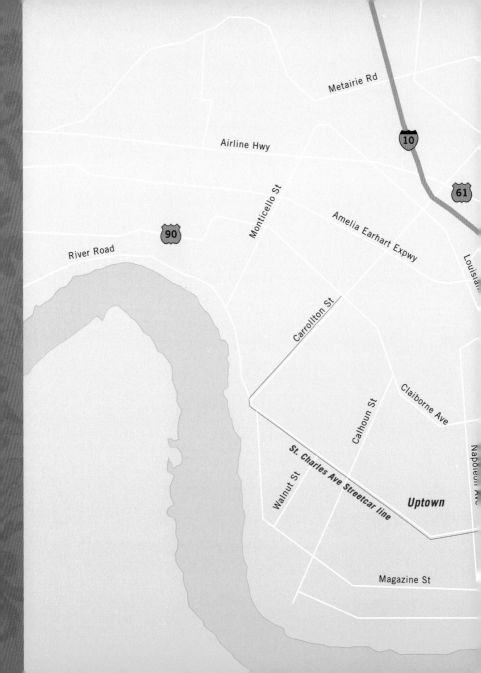

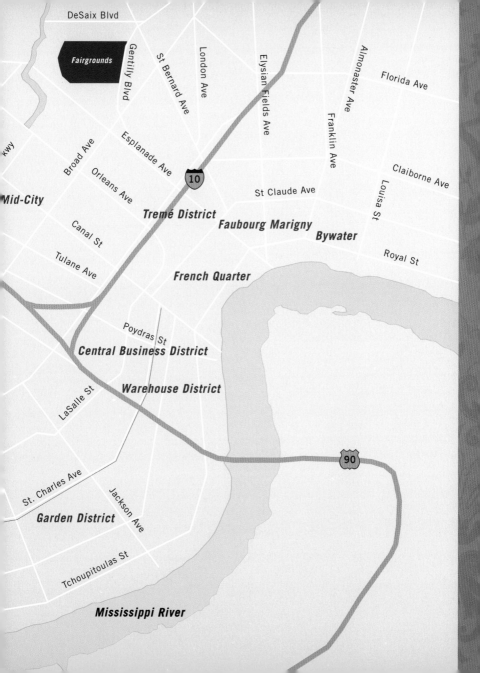

FRENCH QUARTER

New Orleans' most famous neighborhood was its first. Also known as the Vieux Carré ("Old Quarter"), the modern-day French Quarter marks the original settlement laid out in 1718. "The Quarter" is the city's high-profile tourist district, most famous for its historical sights and the notorious Bourbon Street district. Its streets are named for various members of French nobility and their patron saints, and the streets are lined with pristine 18th century Spanish-influenced architecture.

● **DISCOVER THE FOLLOWING LEGENDARY GEMS IN THE FOOD & DRINK AND CLASSICS SECTIONS:**

Food
1. Antoine's
2. Arnaud's
3. Brennan's
4. Café Du Monde
5. Galatoire's
6. Irene's Cuisine
7. Lucky Dogs (on street corners)

Cocktails
8. Carousel Bar at the Monteleon
9. Napoleon House

Hotels
10. Hotel Maison de Ville and Audubon Cottages
11. Monteleone Hotel

Music
12. Donna's
13. Funky Butt on Congo Square
14. House of Blues
15. Preservation Hall

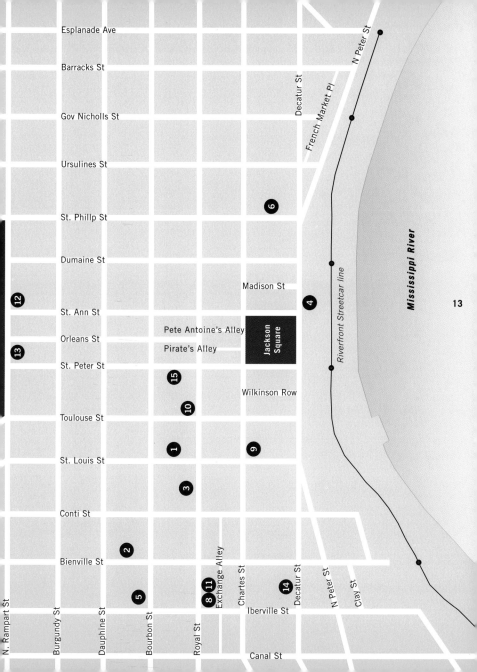

CENTRAL BUSINESS DISTRICT (CBD)
AND THE WAREHOUSE DISTRICT

Immediately upriver from the French Quarter, the Central Business District (CBD) is the city's modern-day office and commercial zone. Known in earlier days as the Faubourg Sainte Marie, the neighborhood was added during the days of Spanish rule and included the rough-and-tumble riverfront docks frequented by frontier tradesmen and traveling roustabouts. The adjacent Warehouse District has recently undergone an upscale facelift with new art galleries, restaurants and museums occupying formerly abandoned industrial space.

● DISCOVER THE FOLLOWING LEGENDARY GEMS IN THE FOOD & DRINK AND CLASSICS SECTIONS:

Food
  Mother's

Hotels
  W New Orleans
  The Whitney
  Windsor Court

Music
  Howlin' Wolf

GARDEN DISTRICT

Hop on the St. Charles streetcar, and you'll roll through the first 'American' section of New Orleans – aptly named the Garden District. In the early to mid-1800s, French Creoles forbade the English-speaking merchants from living in the Vieux Carré, so these wealthy merchants created their own neighborhood of stately mansions that still stand today. The side streets off of St. Charles are filled with architectural gems from the mid-19th century and the haunting crypts of Lafayette Cemetery #1.

● DISCOVER THE FOLLOWING LEGENDARY GEMS IN THE FOOD & DRINK AND CLASSICS SECTIONS:

Hotels
The Whitney Inn

UPTOWN

As the streetcar and urban layout follow the broad arc of the Mississippi, we enter Uptown – the largely residential district that plays home to New Orleans' major universities, the sprawling Audubon Park and its state-of-the-art zoological gardens. Off the main avenues, intrepid explorers can find working-class communities, small-scale commercial districts, student bars, and out-of-the-way neighborhood restaurants frequented by locals, not visiting conventioneers.

● DISCOVER THE FOLLOWING LEGENDARY GEMS IN THE FOOD & DRINK AND CLASSICS SECTIONS:

Food
Casamento's
Dunbar's Creole Cuisine
Franky and Johnnie's
Pascal's Manale

Hotels
The Columns Hotel

Music
Maple Leaf
Tipatina's

FAUBOURG MARIGNY

Just a hop across Esplanade Avenue from the French Quarter, the funky Faubourg Marigny was the city's Third Municipality and early Creole "suburb." Many original palatial homes built by rich Creoles were subdivided into down-market apartments. In recent years, this artist-friendly neighborhood has seen a boom in bed and breakfast inns since it is so close to the Quarter. You'll also find gay culture (clubs and bookstores), and live music venues along a stretch of Frenchmen Street.

● **DISCOVER THE FOLLOWING LEGENDARY GEMS IN THE FOOD & DRINK AND CLASSICS SECTIONS:**

Hotels
Girod House

Music
Snug Harbor

BYWATER

Many of the city's artists, displaced by rising rents in the Marigny, headed to the nearby Bywater. The Bywater is a downscale residential/industrial neighborhood that borders the working-class Ninth Ward. Thanks to the wonders of gentrification, Bywater is now described as "transitional" and real estate prices are inching higher. The neighborhood is home to a few notable, yet hidden, restaurants and music venues

● DISCOVER THE FOLLOWING LEGENDARY GEMS IN THE FOOD & DRINK AND CLASSICS SECTIONS:

Food
Elizabeth's

TREMÉ

Across Rampart Street from the Quarter, the Tremé (pronounced treh-MAY) district is home to the legendary Congo Square and two of the city's oldest cemeteries: St Louis #1 and #2. Traditionally the home of the city's black Creole population, it was also the location of Storyville, New Orleans' infamous row of bars, bordellos and gambling houses at the turn of the 20th century. The residential areas of the Tremé – including several public housing projects – have been beset by poverty in the modern era. Unfortunately, this creates a relatively tourist-hostile environment just blocks from Louis Armstrong's namesake park and the fascinating historical "cities of the dead."

MID CITY/CITY PARK AND FAIRGROUNDS

Away from the river and toward the lake, the Mid-City and City Park districts (formerly "Back of Town") are more recent additions – mostly developed after the Civil War. Present-day Mid-City is a mix of residential and commercial zones. Though it lacks the old world charm of the river neighborhoods, it is home to many of New Orleans' workaday joints such as Mandina's Restaurant, Liuzza's Bar, and the wildly successful Mid City Rock & Bowl. The City Park/Fairground area also plays host to the nearly-overwhelming New Orleans Jazz and Heritage Festival. The last weekend of April and first weekend of May, Jazzfest crowds pack the infield of the Fairgrounds horse track to hear hundreds of local and touring acts in a celebration of local jazz, R&B, hip hop and gospel music.

● DISCOVER THE FOLLOWING LEGENDARY GEMS IN THE FOOD & DRINK AND CLASSICS SECTIONS:

Food
    Liuzza's Lounge and Grill
    (on Lopez St.)
    (a.k.a. Liuzza's By the Track)
    Mandina's

Cocktails
    Liuzza's Bar and Grill
    (on Bienville St.)

Music
    Mid-City Rock and Bowl

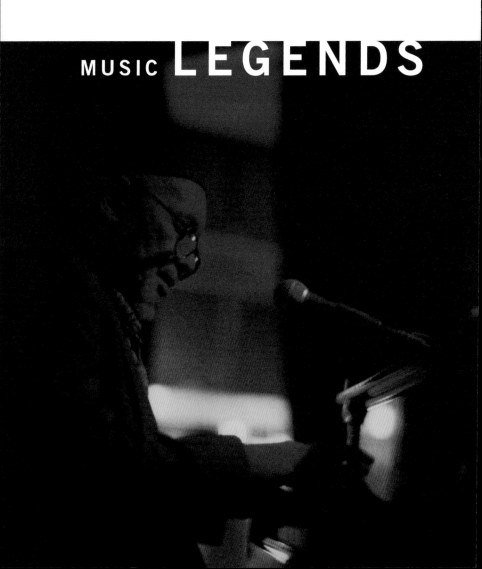

MUSIC LEGENDS

Just as the Mississippi brought goods and settlers to the burgeoning port, the river made New Orleans an American musical capital as well. Over New Orleans' 300-year history, music from the agricultural areas of the Deep South (country blues, African-derived slave chants and Protestant spirituals) was mixed with European traditions (most notably brass band and piano traditions) and even rhythmic influences from the Afro-Caribbean islands. From the blaring jazz trumpet solos to backbeat-heavy rhythm and blues, New Orleans music is as alive and diverse as the city itself.

New Orleans is teaming with music legends – from jazz ambassador Louis Armstrong to Soul Queen Irma Thomas to the Neville's funky family dynasty – all of whom give the Crescent City a high-profile presence on the international music scene.

MUSICAL STYLES THAT DEVELOPED

JAZZ

Long touted as the "birthplace of jazz," New Orleans is at the very least a hotbed of this 20th century American musical form. Musicians who played in the Storyville's red-light district brought the horn-based musical style to the city's black neighborhoods, where it flourished and still thrives. Fans can find examples of nearly every school of jazz performed in the city's clubs, from the intricate, up-tempo Dixieland played at Bourbon Street's Preservation Hall to modern bop-influenced styles championed by the multi-generational Marsalis family.

You could say that after a hundred years, jazz flows through New Orleans' water supply. Whether a local band is playing Jewish folk music or dance-friendly funk, the rhythms and syncopated beats of jazz are close to the surface.

BLUES AND GOSPEL

These twin towers of American roots music cast their distinct shadows on the instrumental and vocal music of New Orleans. While the character and underlying structure of the blues are the basis for much of the city's jazz and soul music, the melodies of the church provided early outlets for many New Orleans artists before they made a jump to more secular tunes.

PIANO STYLES

From the early barrelhouse tunes of Jelly Roll Morton to the rock steady R&B of Fats Domino, masters of the keyboard have long dominated New Orleans music. Wherever you go in the city, you'll hear prime examples of the city's keyboard legacy, from the evergreen tunes of Allen Toussaint to the energetic rolling rhythms of James Booker.

SECOND LINE/BRASS BANDS

New Orleans' street parade traditions – most notably Mardi Gras, funeral processions and gatherings of "Social Aid and Pleasure Clubs" – have left an indelible mark on the city's musical heritage. The traditional post-parade dancing and drumming – the "second line" – followed formal marchers and became a distinctive part of the city's parade-heavy culture. These second lines led to distinctive rhythms that permeate modern New Orleans music. Brass bands that paraded the city's streets in earlier days have been revived by a new generation of local musicians who work jazz and danceable funk into energetic new compositions and traditional tunes alike.

SOUL/BLUES/ RHYTHM & BLUES

And then there's the "holy trinity" of modern New Orleans music – three styles that mix freely and inform just about every act performing in the city today. Powerful vocals, soulful guitar work, and driving rhythms come together in styles that are diverse but still recognizable as New Orleans' own. Suffice it to say, you'll know 'em when you hear 'em.

CAJUN AND ZYDECO

Until recently, these two popular accordion-based styles from rural French Louisiana were relatively rare in New Orleans. However, a booming tourist industry and enthusiasm for all things Louisiana have made urban performances more common.

Known as "chank-a-chank" for its trademark rhythm, **Cajun** music is essentially French-language country music dominated by fiddle and one-row accordion. Two-steps and waltzes are the most common dance steps, but a mournful Cajun fiddle ballad can all but break a listener's heart.

Also sung in French, **zydeco** has a more modern sound – hard-grooving R&B bands fronted by accordion and rubboard. A successful country/city transplant, this home-grown music of Acadiana's Creole communities has become immensely popular in New Orleans and across the nation.

27

THE LEGENDS OF MUSIC

The songs compiled on the *Legends of New Orleans* CD present a cross-section of the city's living musical traditions and are meant to whet the appetite for broader listening or a Jazzfest/nightclub pilgrimage to the city itself. As with any retrospective tribute, the limitations of time and space have prevented the inclusion of all legendary figures in New Orlean's music, including the Marselis family, Jelly Roll Morton and recently departed Ernie K-Doe to name a few. With a single-volume tribute, we can only scratch the surface.

1. It's All Over Now
Dirty Dozen Brass Band with Dr. John

Starting with an upbeat sousaphone groove, "It's All Over Now" kicks off our exploration of the city's music with a funky twist on New Orleans' "second-line" tradition. The Dirty Dozen was among the first local brass bands to thoroughly incorporate contemporary musical influences (bebop, avant-garde jazz and funk) into the rhythmic marching music of neighborhood "Social Aid and Pleasure Clubs." Local boy Mac Rebennack (known more widely as Dr. John) contributes vocals to this Dirty Dozen favorite. Dr. John achieved considerable national fame with his hit "Right Place, Right Time" in the 1970's (during his "psychedelic voodoo priest" phase) and has since become better known as a rootsy traditionalist dedicated to New Orleans' jazz and boogie-woogie keyboard traditions.

2. Blue Monday
Fats Domino

During the early 1950s, Fats Domino's steady-chord keyboard style and distinctive vocals dominated blues, R&B and emerging "rock and roll" radio throughout the US. Recorded in 1955 – the same year as his chart topping theme song "Blueberry Hill" – "Blue Monday" showcases Domino's rock-steady right hand chording over a swooping baritone sax riff.

3. Sing It
Irma Thomas, Marcia Ball, and Tracie Nelson

Propelled by a driving second-line rhythm, "Sing It" features soul vocalist Irma Thomas (the official "Soul Queen of New Orleans"), Marcia Ball and East Texas pianist/vocalist Tracey Nelson in an up-tempo piano boogie with a rump-shaking rumba beat. This tune brings together Thomas' powerful vocals with Ball's and Nelson's quick-fingered "Gulf Coast boogie" piano style. You'll hear nimble barrelhouse piano rolls snake through complex drumbeats throughout the tune.

4. *Amazing Grace*
Neville Brothers

For those of you keeping score at home, there are four original Nevilles: Art, Aaron, Charles and Cyril. The Neville Brothers – dubbed "New Orleans' first family of funk" – are probably best known for their percussive dance tunes and carnival classics that blend the rhythmic influences of reggae, funk, and R&B into a soulful "home-grown world music." Our featured live recording of the old hymn "Amazing Grace" features another side of the Nevilles – a sparse, down-tempo ballad where brother Aaron's soaring falsetto floats over haunting layers of Hammond organ and slow-picked guitar.

5. *On A Night Like This*
Buckwheat Zydeco

There's no mistaking the distinctive sound of south Louisiana's zydeco music – hard-pumping accordion and metallic, offbeat percussion from the froittoir (rubboard) are a dead giveaway. This infectious R&B-based dance music is one of Louisiana's best-known musical exports and Stanley "Buckwheat" Dural is one of its best contemporary practitioners. Pulling double duty on accordion and lead vocals, Buckwheat leads his groove-heavy band through the catchy dance tune.

6. *Do You Know What It Means (To Miss New Orleans)*
Louis Armstrong

This poignant, nostalgic ballad from Louis "Satchmo" Armstrong exemplifies the legendary aspects of New Orleans jazz. Armstrong, a giant of American jazz since the 1920s, was a native of New Orleans and the city's most visible showman and ambassador until his death in 1971. In "Do You Know What It Means" Armstrong demonstrates the scratchy-voiced vocals and powerful, melodic coronet solo style that were his trademarks throughout his near-mythical career.

7. *One Foot in the Bayou*
Filé

Twenty-year veterans of the south Louisiana roots music scene, Lafayette-based Filé (pronounced FEE-lay) combines Cajun and Creole influences in a wide-ranging swamp-pop sound. This tune is a Louisiana case study in "country-come-to-the-city." One Foot in the Bayou tells the story of a Louisiana bayou girl gone to live in New York and features traditional Cajun accordion lines and rollicking barrelhouse piano rolls in a mid-tempo rock and roll shuffle.

8. *High Society*
Pete Fountain

Since in the mid-1950s, clarinetist Pete Fountain has been a high-profile ambassador of New Orleans Dixieland jazz. In the 1960s, the New Orleans native was a regular on such TV shows as Lawrence Welk and the Tonight Show at a time when the local market for Dixieland waned. "High Society" is Fountain's salute to the organized chaos of full-tilt Dixieland jazz. From the first entrance of Fountain's four-piece horn section, it's every man for himself in a breakneck yet intricate display of instrumental virtuosity and showmanship.

9. *(You'll Be) Satisfied*
The Subdudes

The Subdudes gained a nationwide following for a distinctive brand of R&B-influenced pop music during the 1990s. After establishing a loyal fan base in New Orleans, the group relocated to Colorado and broke up after their 1997 album "Live at Last." In this tune from 1994's "Annunciation," smooth guitar lines nod to the upriver influence of the seminal Memphis Stax/Volt soul, and Tommy Malone's unrestrained vocals bring a gospel-like feel to the Subdudes Louisiana-inspired music.

10. New Orleans, My Home Town
Al Hirt

Trumpeter Al Hirt – a Crescent City standby and contemporary of clarinetist Pete Fountain – offered this now-campy homage to New Orleans during the 1960s. It's a particular strain of Dixieland-influenced "easy listening" fare – the music of New Orleans run through a Vegas/California filter, then layered with a highly-polished backup chorus. Anyone familiar with the funky undercurrent common to New Orleans music would have a hard time recognizing the "wear a happy smile, that's the style" town described here.

11. Congo Square
Sonny Landreth

Another Acadiana underground legend, slide guitarist Sonny Landreth has lent his powerful and eclectic sound to acts as diverse as songwriter John Hiatt and the late king of zydeco Clifton Chenier. In his period piece "Congo Square" Landreth juxtaposes his own moody slide guitar stylings with an unrelenting jungle drumbeat that hearkens back to the early days of Code Noir-era New Orleans. From start to finish, strong percussion drives the tune and pays respect to New Orleans' first infusion of African culture – with all its attendant mystery and voodoo-related mysticism. In the forefront, Landreth puts his guitar through a diverse set of paces – from grungy, distorted chords that mimic the drums to solos that echo tortured wails in the night.

12. *Black Satin*
Katie Webster

The late blues pianist Katie Webster kicks off her instrumental "Black Satin" with a two-handed THUMP, and doesn't let up until the song's final chords. Another Texas-born keyboard phenomenon and veteran of Otis Redding's late-60s band, Webster held the title "Swamp Boogie Queen" for her powerful two-fisted piano style that incorporated R&B, south Louisiana swamp pop and driving boogie-woogie piano styles. In "Black Satin," Webster is in classic form; with steady boogie bass lines played against strong, tinkling melody lines in the upper registers.

13. *St. Louis Blues*
Preservation Hall Jazz Band

Four hours a night, seven nights a week, the Dixieland veterans of Preservation Hall still put on a hell of a good show. A customary stop for Bourbon Street first-timers, Preservation Hall still draws constant crowds in search of the authentic sounds of "trad jazz," appropriately played by artists in their eighties. This bouncy version of "St. Louis Blues" alternates spirited solos (trumpet, clarinet, piano and swooping trombone) with communal free-for-all choruses.

14. Go to the Mardi Gras
Professor Longhair

Henry Roeland Byrd, more widely known as Professor Longhair, was the author of this rollicking Mardi Gras anthem as well as a primary architect of the New Orleans keyboard style. Carnival pilgrims are usually familiar with a litany of the Professor's tunes, among them "Carnival Time" and "Tipatina." Local piano players influenced by "Fess" are too numerous to mention, but suffice it to say that Longhair's legacy lives on through such musical luminaries as James Booker and Huey "Piano" Smith and their legions of disciples. Every year, between Twelfth Night and Fat Tuesday, "Go to the Mardi Gras" is in constant radio rotation, complete with its locomotive snare, bouncing piano riffs, and the warbling whistle of the Professor himself.

15. Heaven is the Place I Want to Be
Raymond Myles

A shining example of the power-gospel form, Raymond A. Myles' "Heaven is the Place" is a sweetly-sung sermon backed by one of New Orleans' finest mass choirs. A long-standing crowd pleaser at Jazzfest's Gospel Tent, Myles was known for his energetic live performances, strong compositions, and impassioned solo vocals. As the leader of the RAMS (Raymond A. Myles Singers), Myles was a legend of the New Orleans gospel scene, performing regularly for local churches and music festivals. With its intricate "preacher style" vocals, "Heaven is a Place" showcases Myles at his peak of spiritual showmanship. His life was cut short in 1998 by an inner-city carjacking in his hometown of New Orleans.

FOOD & **DRINK**

As any dedicated food fan can tell you, the legendary culture of New Orleans isn't limited to nightclubs or street parades. The Crescent City boasts one of the most active food scenes in the country (if not the world). It's known as a restaurant city where it's literally hard to find a less-than-stellar meal – whether you're paying top dollar at a white-tablecloth establishment or forking out three bucks for a generously stuffed oyster poboy.

Creole cuisine – the city's sophisticated, butter-rich cooking style – is essentially Continental French cuisine adapted to the ingredients of the New World. As with the city's music traditions, the flow of immigrants and native ingredients influenced the city's edible cultures and resulted in a uniquely stellar, food-crazed metropolis. New Orleans food shows the contributions of French, African, Spanish, Italian and Croatian cooks, served up in a style that's as unique as the city itself.

Culinary traditions from the other parts of Louisiana also thrive in New Orleans. The rustic frontier foods of south Louisiana's Cajun population came to the city and burst onto the scene in the 1980s, while soul food common to the Deep South also ranks high in the edible pantheon.

BLUE MARBLE MENU SPECIALS
NEW ORLEANS

The following Menu Specials provide a "culinary cheat sheet" of New Orleans' classic dishes as well as recommendations of a great place in the city to experience each dish.

BEIGNETS AND CAFÉ AU LAIT

New Orleans' answer to the breakfast doughnut, the beignet is a crispy, puffy square of deep fried dough sprinkled liberally with powdered sugar. In between dusty bites, sip a smooth café au lait (equal parts strong coffee and hot milk). In the city, dark-roasted coffee is often mixed with roasted chicory – an herb root related to andive resulting in the distinctively flavored 'New Orleans blend'. Originally, chicory was added to extend scarce coffee beans.

Café Du Monde (French Quarter) 1039 Decatur St. 504.587.0835

BARBECUE SHRIMP

Despite the misleading name, New Orleans' barbecue shrimp never go near a smoky grill. Instead, these heads-on crustaceans are baked or sautéed in an addictive butter sauce that's heavily spiced with Worcestershire, garlic and black pepper. The original recipe has been tracked back to Pascal's Manale on Napoleon Avenue. Now the dish shows up on countless menus across town. Eaten correctly, these plump beauties require a bib for shirtfront protection (a common practice among local executives) and countless loaves of bread for "sopping up the gravy."

Pascal's Manale (Uptown) 1838 Napoleon Ave. 504.895.4877

GUMBO

When Louisiana's winter turns cold and wet, locals refer to the climate as "good gumbo weather." Somewhere between flavorful stew and thick soup, hearty Louisiana gumbo can be made with anything from seasonal Gulf seafood (plump oysters, partially-shelled crabs or peeled shrimp) to wild duck and Cajun sausage. Hank Williams fans may ask for filé (FEE-lay) gumbo thickened with ground sassafras leaves, but every Louisiana cook has his or her own version of this dish – some thickened with okra, some with a dark roux, and others even flavored with tomato (a New Orleans tradition).

Liuzza's Lounge and Grill (Midcity)
(a.k.a. "Liuzza's by the track")
1518 N. Lopez St. 504.943.8667

JAMBALAYA

Jambalaya (pronounced johm-buh-LIE-uh) is a rice-based dish loosely based on Spain's paella tradition – white rice cooked in a simmering stew of seafood, pork, or chicken. The rice soaks up the juices from the meats, and the result is a perfect one-pot meal. Though there are no hard and fast rules about the ingredients, jambalaya is a great "clean-out-the-fridge" dish often flecked with chunks of poultry, shrimp or peeled crawfish tails. The Spanish term for ham ("jamón") puts the "jam" in jambalaya, though oftentimes slices of spicy andouille sausage are substituted. Creole cooks in New Orleans are known to add tomato to their jambalaya, though purist Cajun cooks usually cook theirs without.

Mother's (CBD) 401 Poydras 504.523.9656

CRAWFISH

Once considered a food of Louisiana's rural poor, crawfish (known elsewhere as crayfish) are a strain of crustacean that flourishes in the swamps and wetlands of the state. Resembling tiny freshwater lobsters, crawfish are revered for their flavorful tail meat which is somewhere between shrimp and lobster in taste and texture. The peak "live" season for crawfish is late spring, when local wetlands warm up from the winter chill. In the off-season, peeled crawfish tails can be found in crawfish etouffee (tails smothered in gravy) and crawfish bisque (a roux-based soup garnished with stuffed crawfish heads).

Franky and Johnnie's (Uptown) 321 Arabella 504.899.9146

TROUT MUNIERE

In the 1980s, Paul Prudhomme's spicy blackened redfish became New Orleans' most trendy fish dish, but traditionalists stick by this more classic Creole preparation – fresh Gulf fish in a brown butter sauce. The technique couldn't be simpler or more tasty – delicate speckled trout filets are quickly pan-fried (or paneed) and topped with a cooked sauce of butter, lemon and fresh parsley. A close cousin – trout amandine – is the muniere with an added layer of crispy slivered almonds.

Galatoire's (French Quarter) 209 Bourbon St. 504.525.2021
(Pronounced GAL-uh-twahz)

Mandina's (Midcity) 3800 Canal St. 504.482.9179

RED BEANS AND RICE

A simple take on the universal "rice and beans" motif, red beans are slow-cooked with aromatic vegetables (onion, celery, green pepper and garlic) until smooth and silky, then served over a bed of white rice. Traditionally, the dish started with the leftover hambone from Sunday dinner and was a perfect low-maintenance meal for Monday, which was local laundry day before the advent of automated washer/dryer combos. Modern versions can be flavored with ham or chunks of spicy smoked sausage.

Dunbar's Creole Cuisine (Uptown) 4927 Robert St. 504.899.0734

OYSTERS

It seems that every other storefront in New Orleans includes the phrase "Oyster Bar" on its sign. And with good reason – the Gulf of Mexico's oyster beds produce millions of these fresh, rocky mollusks every year. Belly up to one of the city's countless "raw bars" and order a dozen on the half shell – during the winter and early spring, they're fat, salty and at their seasonal peak. Over the years, experimental Creole chefs have also tried their hand at baking these plump bivalves and come up with classics such as Oysters Rockefeller (oysters mixed with chopped spinach, onion, bread crumbs and Herbsaint, then baked on the half shell) and Oysters Bienville (with shrimp and a delicate wine sauce).

Casamento's (Uptown) 4330 Magazine St. 504.895.9761

Arnaud's (French Quarter) 813 Bienville St. 504.523.5433

SHRIMP REMOULADE

Spicy or creamy, this cold-sauced dish can be topped with a horseradish-spiked tomato sauce or a mayo-like dressing. Either way, the shrimp will be tender beauties from the nearby Gulf. A good remoulade appetizer is God's vision of the perfect shrimp cocktail.

Uglesich's (CBD/Warehouse) 1238 Baronne 504.523.8571
(Caveats: Lunch only. Cash only. Expect a wait.)

THE POBOY

Alternately known as the "poor boy," this huge sandwich is ever-present and a great value for your walking-food dollar. Monstrous loaves of fresh local French bread (usually 9-12 inches in length) are stuffed with any manner of fillings – from gravy-soaked roast beef to fresh-fried shrimp tails or meatballs drenched in marinara sauce (called "red gravy" in the local Yat lingo). In the neighborhoods, just about every corner grocery doubles as a makeshift sandwich counter, so keep your eyes open for handwritten signs ("POBOYS TODAY") in unlikely shop windows.

Elizabeth's (Bywater) 601 Gallier 504.944.9272
(Try the "french fry and gravy" poboy.)

BREAD PUDDING WITH BOURBON SAUCE

A perpetual item on every restaurant's dessert list, this rich confection transforms day-old bread into a tasty custard of egg, sugar and cream. The common topping for bread pudding is a hot, sugary sauce spiked with a shot of bourbon, though some chefs prefer to tempt diners with praline or white chocolate toppings.

Irene's Cuisine (French Quarter) 539 St. Philip St. 504.529.8811

BANANAS FOSTER

Another classic New Orleans dessert, this dish combines butter-sautéed bananas with deep brown sugar, banana liqueurs, spices and a healthy shot of high-proof rum. The result is a rich, syrupy goop served on rich ice cream. In its natural habitat (the upscale Creole restaurant), Bananas Foster is a show unto itself – prepared tableside with a flourish and a roaring four-foot flame.

Brennan's (French Quarter) 417 Royal St. 504.525.9713

NEW ORLEANS COCKTAILS

The French Quarter abounds with barkers hawking 3-for-1 beers, foot-tall frozen daiquiris, and other near-flammable tourist drinks, but the classic cocktails of New Orleans aren't pumped out of high octane Slurpee machines. (An occasional mind-erasing rum drink might be a pleasant Bourbon Street diversion, but stringent Drunk Tourist Code requires that you sip them from slender plastic alien-shaped receptacles.) For a more measured approach to the inebriational arts, ask the bartender to pour one of these refined concoctions.

SAZERAC

Whiskey drinkers should belly up to this bourbon-based cocktail as a close cousin of the Old Fashioned. Sweetened with simple syrup and flavored with two different kinds of aromatic bitters, the Sazerac is usually served straight up or on the rocks. For an authentic version, a chilled glass is rinsed with a few drops of Herbsaint. Bonus points for old-guy bartenders who give you a more advanced alternative: "Rye whiskey or bourbon?". Try one of each (over a few hours) and compare.

Napoleon House (French Quarter) 500 Chartres St. 504.524.9752

PIMM'S CUP

When you need a good cooling off, try this local alternative to the gin and tonic. The active ingredient – Pimm's No. 1 – is a gin-based aperitif made by (of all people) the English. This tasty highball calls for a shot of Pimm's over ice topped up with a bubbly soft drink of your choosing (lemon-lime, ginger ale, or straight soda). The lemon slice won't raise any eyebrows, but the other traditional garnish – a spear or round of cucumber – just might be a surprise.

The Columns Hotel (Uptown) 3811 St. Charles Avenue 504.899.9308

CAFÉ BRULOT

This potent, flaming cocktail is cleverly disguised as an elaborate after-dinner coffee drink. A bowlful of brandy is spiced with cloves and citrus, then torched to a blue flame, mixed for the sake of a good show and finally extinguished with a stream of hot chicory coffee.

Antoine's (French Quarter) 713 St. Louis St. 504.581.4422
(the city's oldest serving restaurant)

BLOODY MARY

As you might expect for such a hard-drinking town, New Orleans has its own take on this classic hangover helper. The local version of the vodka/tomato drink is usually plenty strong, liberally spiced with various pepper concoctions, and chock full of crunchy pickled vegetables (green beans or okra). Don't ask. Just drink…

The Carousel Bar at the Monteleone Hotel (French Quarter)
214 Royal St. 504.523.3341

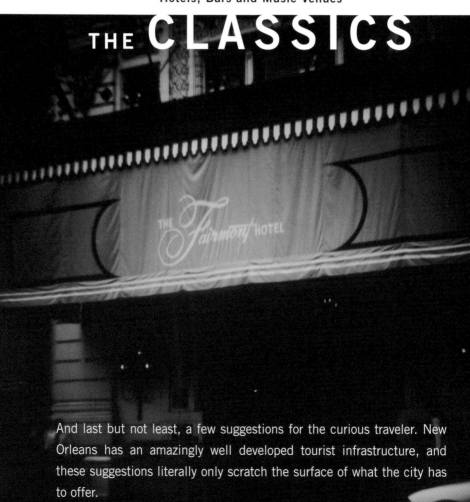

Hotels, Bars and Music Venues

THE CLASSICS

And last but not least, a few suggestions for the curious traveler. New Orleans has an amazingly well developed tourist infrastructure, and these suggestions literally only scratch the surface of what the city has to offer.

HOTELS

The Columns (Uptown)
3811 St. Charles Avenue
504.899.9308
Converted St. Charles mansion provides
opulence and one of the city's best bars.

Girod House Bed and Breakfast
(Faubourg Marigny)
835 Esplenade 504.944.7993,
toll free 866.877-1024
Comfortable suites with kitchens
in a renovated Creole hideaway.

Hotel Maison de Ville and
Audubon Cottages (French Quarter)
727 Toulouse St. 504.561.5858
Swank, historical and romantic digs
in the midst of the Quarter. The nearby
Audubon Cottages are a hidden
(if pricey) local treasure.

Monteleone (French Quarter)
214 Royal St. 504.523.3341
Sprawling upscale French Quarter
institution, in business since the 1880s.

W New Orleans (CBD)
333 Poydras 504.525.9444
Twenty-three floors of stylish,
upscale accommodations.

The Whitney Hotel (CBD)
610 Poydras 504.581.4222
A New Orleans bank-turned-hotel
recently renovated by the
Wyndham chain.

47

The Whitney Inn (Garden District)
1509 St. Charles Avenue
504.821.8000
Renovated 1800s charm on the city's
grand avenue.

Windsor Court (CBD)
300 Gravier St. 504.523.6000
A renowned luxury hotel just steps
from the French Quarter.

Fairmont Hotel (CBD)
123 Baronne 504.529-7111
Old school luxury in the near-Quarter CBD.

BARS AND MUSIC VENUES

Donna's (French Quarter)
800 North Rampart St. 504.596.6914
Brass band ground zero.

Funky Butt on Congo Square
(French Quarter)
225 North Rampart St. 504.558.0872
Newish jazz club across from
Armstrong Park.

House of Blues (French Quarter)
255 Decatur 504.529.2583
The reigning 800-pound gorilla of the
local music scene. Good balance of local
groups and road acts.

Howlin' Wolf
(CBD/Warehouse District)
828 St. Peters St. 504.522-9653
Jazz and blues in the Warehouse District.

Liuzza's (Uptown)
3636 Bienville St. 504.482.9120
Famous for their "frozen bowling balls of
beer," Liuzza's is a classic Midcity bar
with an outstanding Creole/Italian kitchen
in the back.

Maple Leaf (Uptown)
8316 Oak St. 504.866.9359
Eclectic booking (from brass to zydeco
and back) keeps this Riverbend club
hopping.

Mid-City Rock and Bowl (Mid City)
4133 South Carrolton 504.482.3133
Zydeco and R&B in a renovated
bowling alley.

49

Preservation Hall (French Quarter)
726 St. Peter St. 504.523.8939
The classic tourist venue for Dixieland
veterans.

Snug Harbor (Faubourg Marigny)
626 Frenchmen St. 504.949-0696
The city's best club for post-Dixieland jazz.

Tipatina's (Uptown)
501 Napoleon 504.895.8477
The mythical Uptown club that launched
countless local legends.

FESTIVAL **SCHEDULE**

MARDI GRAS

Carnival season runs from January 6th (Twelfth Night on the Catholic liturgical calendar) to the moveable feast of Mardi Gras (Fat Tuesday). The climactic big day can fall anywhere from early February to the second week of March, so check your local listings before booking a flight.

NEW ORLEANS JAZZ AND HERITAGE FESTIVAL (AKA: JAZZFEST)

New Orleans' springtime celebration of its music, food, and crafts. Recent years have brought more high-dollar road acts and attendant crowds. Held on the last weekend of April and the first weekend of May.

FRENCH QUARTER FESTIVAL

Touted as a smaller, more local version of Jazzfest, but the tourist crowds have already caught on. Memorial Day weekend.

FESTIVAL INTERNATIONAL DE LOUISIANE

Outstanding world music festival in the Acadiana's hub city of Lafayette. Musicians, dancers and visual artists from the four corners of the French-speaking world. Last weekend of April.

ADDITIONAL RESOURCES

COOKBOOKS

Jambalaya – Junior League of New Orleans
Classic New Orleans recipes from the "ladies who lunch".

Who's Your Mama, Are You Catholic, and Can You Make a Roux?
– Marcelle Bienvenue
A wealth of Cajun recipes and family tales from one of South
Louisiana's best cook/storytellers.

RADIO

WWOZ (90.7 FM)
Also known simply as "O.Z.", this community sponsored FM
station plays ALL the diverse music of New Orleans and is
ground zero for local music fans.

WODT (1280 AM)
All blues all the time.

LITERATURE

Confederacy of Dunces – John Kennedy Toole
Comedic classic of neighborhood New Orleans starring the
unpleasantly hilarious Ignatius J. Reilly.

The Moviegoer – Walker Percy
An atmospheric, haunting novel set in 1950s New Orleans.

LOCAL PRINT MEDIA

Gambit Weekly
The city's free alternative weekly contains solid local news and comprehensive music and event listings. Publishes on Sunday.

Best of New Orleans
Intended for out-of-towners, BONO is a glossy, free monthly magazine from the Gambit people.

Times-Picayune
The town's established daily newspaper. The Entertainment insert is published in Friday's issue.

WWWEB RESOURCES

www.neworleanscvb.com
The online home of the New Orleans Convention and Visitor's Bureau (CVB). Full of local information and online hotel booking.

www.offbeat.com
Local music magazine (Offbeat) on the web. Easy-to-use live music calendar allows you to search by date, neighborhood, and musical style.

www.neworleans.citysearch.com
This full-featured city guide lists profiles of local hotels, restaurants, and events.

www.jazznethotels.com
A local discount hotel broker with easy search functions and local deals.

MUSIC CREDITS

1. *IT'S ALL OVER NOW* 4:56
(Bobby Womack/Shirley Womack)
The Dirty Dozen Brass Band
℗ 1989 Sony Music Entertainment Inc.
Under license from Sony Music Special Products

2. *BLUE MONDAY* 2:14
(Domino/Bartholomew)
Fats Domino
Courtesy EMI Records,
Under license from EMI-Capitol Music Special Markets

3. *SING IT* 4:17
(David Egan)
Irma Thomas, Marcia Ball and Tracy Nelson
℗ 1998 Rounder Records Corp.
Courtesy of Rounder Records

4. *AMAZING GRACE (LIVE)* 3:14
(Public Domain/Arranged by Aaron Neville)
The Neville Brothers
℗ 1994 A&M Records
Courtesy of A&M Records
Under license from Universal Music Enterprises

5. *ON A NIGHT LIKE THIS* 2:32
(Bob Dylan)
Buckwheat Zydeco
℗ 1987 The Island Def Jam Music Group
Courtesy of The Island Def Jam Music Group
Under license from Universal Music Enterprises

6. *DO YOU KNOW WHAT IT MEANS TO MISS NEW ORLEANS?* 2:59
(L. Alter/E. Delange)
Louis Armstrong and his Orchestra
All Rights Reserved By BMG Entertainment
Courtesy of RCA Records Label
Affiliate Label: BMG/RCA Catalog

7. *ONE FOOT IN THE BAYOU* 2:43
(D. Egan)
Filé
℗ 1996 Green Linnet Records
Courtesy of Green Linnet Records

8. *HIGH SOCIETY* 5:42
(Steele/Melrose)
Bourbon Street All Star Dixielanders
All Rights Reserved By BMG Entertainment
Courtesy of RCA Records Label,
Affiliate Label: BMG/RCA Catalog

9. *(YOU'LL BE) SATISFIED* 3:54
(The Subdudes)
The Subdudes
℗ 1994 Windham Hill Records
Courtesy of Windam Hill

10. *NEW ORLEANS, MY HOME TOWN* 2:14
(Beasley Smith/Teddy Bart)
Al Hirt with Orchestra and Chorus
All Rights Reserved By BMG Entertainment
Courtesy of RCA Records Label,
Affiliate Label: BMG/RCA Catalog

11. *CONGO SQUARE* 6:20
(Sonny Landreth/David Ranson/Roy Melton)
Sonny Landreth
℗ 1995 Volcano Entertainment II, L.L.C.
Sonny Landreth appears courtesy of
Volcano Entertainment II, L.L.C.
Affiliate Label: Zoo Entertainment

12. *BLACK SATIN* 3:45
(Webster)
Katie Webster
From the Alligator release "The Swamp Boogie Queen"
℗ 1988 Alligator Records & Artist Mgt., Inc.
Courtesy of Alligator Records

13. *ST. LOUIS BLUES* 5:45
(William C. Handy)
Preservation Hall Jazz Band
℗ 1982 Sony Music Entertainment Inc.
Under license from Sony Music Special Products

14. *GO TO THE MARDI GRAS* 2:47
(H.R. Byrd/Tee Terry)
Professor Longhair
Courtesy of Rounder Records

15. *HEAVEN IS THE PLACE I WANT TO BE* 5:21
(Raymond Myles/Rance Allen)
Raymond Myles
℗ 1996 NYNO Records
Courtesy of NYNO Records used by permission

CREDITS

MUSIC SELECTION: JODY DENBERG AND DENNIS CONSTANTINE

EDITOR: JANE TANNER

MUSIC LICENSING AND MANUFACTURING: BMG SPECIAL PRODUCTS

PHOTOGRAPHY: SHANNON MCINTYRE

PRODUCED BY: STEVE STONE   DESIGN: GILES DESIGN INC.

THE AUTHOR

Your author experiencing barbecue shrimp at Pascal's Manale.

Pableaux Johnson is a New Orleans based food/travel writer and the author of Lonely Planet's World Food New Orleans. As a native of Louisiana's Cajun country and a largely migratory wiseass, Pableaux routinely eats his way through the world's great food cultures and maintains the food/travel website, www.bayoudog.com.

www.bluemarblemusic.com 1/800-860-9442